ISBN: 978-0-9987609-0-2

MATERNALLY CHALLENGED

*HOW MY SPECIAL NEEDS SON TAUGHT
ME TO SACK UP AND LAUGH!*

———

By Kathy Chlan
Founder of Unfiltered Mom

To my husband Robbie and my boys Casey and Christian. Thank you for making me laugh through this wonderful life we have. I love you all to the moon and back!

Also, for always giving me so much material to write about.

TABLE OF CONTENTS

A LETTER TO MY YOUNGER SELF................................1

WHAT THE HELL IS GROWING INSIDE ME?......................5

A LETTER FROM MY TWIN SISTER.........................13

WHAT WAS I THINKING? MISERY LOVES COMPANY....17

A LETTER FROM MY MOTHER................................21

ANYONE ENJOY PROJECTILE VOMITING?.........................23

A LETTER FROM MY BROTHER...............................29

LET'S RIDE ON THE LITTLE YELLOW SCHOOL BUS.......33

ONE MORE LETTER FROM MY MOTHER...........................41

AND HERE COMES THE FOOD THROWING!...................43

LET'S SAY "HI" TO EINSTEIN.......................................49

A LETTER FROM MY HUSBAND.............................55

COULDN'T YOU HAVE STAYED IN THERE
UNTIL YOUR DUE DATE?......................................57

MEET BUBBLES..65

A LETTER FROM MY YOUNGEST SON.................................75

FEELING HIS OATS..77

A LETTER FROM CASEY'S TEACHER.......................83

THE MAYOR IS ELECTED...87

THE MAN HE BECAME...93

A LETTER FROM CASEY..99

A LETTER TO MY YOUNGER SELF

Dear Younger Self,

Where should I begin? Should I give sound advice about what's going to happen in your life? Or should I just let crap hit the fan without any chance of sticking? Or just cut the bullshit and give it to you straight from the heart? I choose the last option. Here goes nothing!

First things first: You are definitely going to have to fight for what you want. And you certainly will not run away from adversity; you will embrace it with open arms. There will be times where you feel like the walls are closing in on you, but you will wholeheartedly push that steel door open. Superman has nothing on you!

On the mistakes front: You won't falter from 'em because you are gonna make a shitload of mistakes. But one attribute that will serve you well is that fighting spirit.

You used to get into fights to protect your sister. Use some of that fire for yourself.

As a mother, there will be times—too many to count—when you want to run away from home. Buying new suitcases will become a ritual. There is also a possibility that your children will have to enter therapy. (So start saving now for that.) You will pray for perfect children, but that will be your own interpretation of what is perfect. Take it from me and lower your expectations for that subject. Just be happy with what you got.

Life will throw you many curveballs, but you will just have to get a bigger bat. Remember: There is no crying in baseball or life. Out of all the tools and coping mechanisms in the world, there will be one thing you use most: the ability to laugh.

Laughter will become your best friend. After all, laughing is so much better than crying. When you are laughing at inappropriate times and people are looking at you, don't pay attention. Turn the other cheek and keep laughing. (One thing: Never forget your Depends! That is a whole other letter about your bodily functions as you age. Another time.)

You will give your children this gift of laughter. They will be strong because of this and—no worries—think you are a good mother. A little "crazy," but good.

So, enjoy this ride we call life, no matter how messy it is! Live, love, laugh and most of all, you are never too old to carpe diem.

Love,

Your older self (or the ol' battle ax)

WHAT THE HELL IS GROWING INSIDE ME?

Most girls grow up with this image in their minds of their wedding day. It is one of a beautiful girl in a fabulous dress walking arm-in-arm with her father. At the end of the aisle is her very own Prince Charming!

I really never thought about mine. I was just trying to get through life as a young girl unfazed. Well, I should have really thought about it, 'cause mine came very fast.

I got married at the age of 25 to one of my brother's very good friends. My brother got remarried, and we were in the wedding together. I had known my husband Robbie since I was four years old. Robbie is eight years older and seemed to always be around. I think some people were shocked and surprised, but I didn't care. He saw me at the stage in life where puberty sets in: that awkward time when you feel mirrors are your worst enemy.

We dated only six months before we got engaged, and in another six months we were married. Our wedding day was a total disaster. (That is another story in itself). Robbie got deathly ill, and I had to attend my wedding alone. I had to cut the cake with my whole bridal party, and my brother took the garter off my leg. Okay, that was weird, but believe me: at that point I really couldn't have cared less. I was drunk and wanted the night to be over. One of the few highlights was going to each individual table and saying, "Thanks for coming. My husband is upstairs violently vomiting as we speak." I maybe should have taken it as a sign or something. LOL.

Fast forward to three months after our honeymoon. I was working in New York City at the Marriott Marquis in the catering department. Mind you, I had a journalism degree and was pounding the pavement to get into the field, but I needed a job, and my brother was the executive chef there, so it worked out. Also, Robbie was such an advocate for me following my dreams. Oh, to be young and naive!

I began to get sick every morning on the bus into the city. Never did it cross my mind that I could be pregnant. I was responsible and on the pill. We had talked about waiting and enjoying married life for a year. As the saying goes, "You plan and God laughs." Well, he must have been wetting his pants.

I took a pregnancy test, and it was positive. I cried for hours because I was so not ready to be a mom. I thought, "Oh, crap. This kid will be in therapy its whole life." I remember going to tell my parents. Some of you may understand the weight of this. I grew up with an Irish Catholic father who was strict with my twin sister and me. We had a curfew and absolutely no boys were ever allowed in our room. Regardless, I think deep down he knew that I, of all people, was not a virgin when I got married. It wasn't that I was bad, but I was always the one girl who would have no problem trying things first. (Read into this however you want.)

We sat down at the kitchen table, and I proceeded to say (as my face was twitching), "I have some great news. I'm pregnant." I looked over at my father, and he was counting on his fingers. My mother Joannie said, "Casey, seriously. She was not a virgin when she got married." I started to laugh, because I knew exactly what he was doing. My dad was checking to see if I had made it to the wedding night. In fact, I really think I was pregnant before. The poor guy was still hoping that I would have a chance to make it into heaven.

I continued to commute into New York City to my job. Every morning I would puke on the bus. You've got to love morning sickness. God must be a man to have invented this! I would bring a brown bag with me to have somewhere to throw up or, to put it eloquently, "toss my cookies."

One morning, when I was four months pregnant, I got on the bus without the bag. A gentleman in a great black suit sat next to me. All of a sudden, I could not control it. It was like the devil was entering my body, and I was waiting for my head to start spinning. What came out of me was both foul and disgusting. And guess where it landed? Right on the Armani model sitting next to me. I began to violently cry and sob, and this poor guy was just so kind about it. I told him I would pay for the cleaning, but he said, "Don't worry about it." I bet this guy wished he had taken another bus leading to hell.

One day, when I was five months pregnant, I was going down the escalator at Port Authority. I started seeing double of everything, and for those who have been to Port Authority and have seen what hangs out there, this is not a good thing. I was almost to the bottom when I went down. As I came to, with an assortment of businessmen walking around me, I sat up. I proceeded to look into the eyes of a very smelly homeless man who was holding a brown paper bag. You can guess what was in that bag, and I so wanted a swig. The man grabbed my hand and helped me up. I leaned against the wall, and he said, "Marilyn, are you okay?" I *loved* this man, and at that time, he was my knight in shining armor. I say, "Thank you so much, but my name is Kathy." He said, "No, you are Marilyn Monroe." Are you kidding me? LOL. I loved him more and handed him fifty dollars.

The next week, the doctor put me out of work. At this time, I hadn't gained that much weight and was sick constantly. Okay, I can hear the women groaning as soon as I put this out there. They are probably cursing me out and saying, "Oh, poor Kathy, not gaining any weight!" Well, I would have given *anything* to have not been sick and allowed to stuff my face with whatever I wanted. This is the only time a woman gets a free pass to be a heffa, so I would have loved to have gotten large.

I was not the kind of girl who warmed up to this pregnancy thing. I didn't love it. When I got pregnant and told my brother, Bobby, his response was, "The wrong sister is having kids first." I was not insulted because he was right and had summed up the whole event for me.

Also, all this talk about your boobs getting bigger? I think that, for me, was the light at the end of the tunnel. I was not well-endowed and was still waiting to get out of a training bra. Well, guess what? My boobs never got bigger, and I never went up a bra size. Are you kidding me? Sure I was disappointed, but think of my husband's devastation. I think he thought I was gonna turn into a porn star and would finally look like a woman. Come to find out, my milk never came in.

On October 2, 1992, at 6:30 a.m., my water broke. As I was lying on my bed, I heard this incredible popping noise, and then the flood gates opened. I never thought, for a first child, that I would go exactly on my due date. I wanted to hold this baby in as long as possible. The less time to screw it up, the better. Back then, my husband had a beeper. (Yes, people, a beeper.) I beeped him, and he called me. Robbie worked about 35 minutes from home, and I was scared to death.I called my mother, and she called my brother, and they both came over.

As I was sitting on the toilet, stark naked with water pouring out, my brother appeared in the bathroom. I started to laugh, because I was naked and he saw me, but then I thought, "Who gives a shit?" All he said was, "Nice." I said, "This is what you are gonna see when Janice goes into labor." My sister-in-law was due in January. I told him to go poke his eyes out and began to laugh. Telling my twin sister was hysterical. She could not believe that Bobby had seen my va-jay-jay. I told her you could not see past the mound holding it up. She was appalled by the whole thing.

Casey Robert Chlan was born at 3:48 p.m. and weighed eight pounds, 20 ounces. He was 19 inches long. In the end, I had to have a C-section, because his head was too big. I thought, "Oh, my God. I hope he doesn't have my head." My brother had given me the nickname of "Heady Ho Ho," because he said that when I was little all you zoomed in on was my head. And they wonder why I needed therapy all those years.

I wanted to try breastfeeding Casey, but I didn't think I could. Remember, my boobs never got bigger. So, at the hospital, a La Leche specialist came in the room. She pulled my gown open and started pulling on my nipples. She was addressing my husband on what to do, and he had this enormous smile on his face. This was already uncomfortable, but guess who was also in the room: my father! I looked over, and he had this blank stare on his face like he wanted to poke his eyes out. When the nurse left, my mother started to laugh. She said, "Call the cardiologist because your father is having a stroke." He sat there for about ten minutes not saying a word. Poor guy!

The journey of becoming a mother was not an easy ride for me, and to be honest, I didn't immediately know what all the fuss was about. I knew that I loved Casey to death, but bonding with him did not come right away.

MATERNALLY CHALLENGED

A LETTER FROM MY TWIN SISTER

The question that always seems to follow twins throughout their lives is: What's it like to be a twin?

When you are a twin, that question always stumps you. It's like a really detailed joke, when at the end you look around to see if anyone else gets it and it looks like no one does.

For years you try to answer it. First, in detail: You give every little story or event to try to explain, even if no one understands it. Then as you get older, you answer a little rushed, giving quick comical snippets of your lives together. By the time you become "yourself" and are comfortable in your own skin, you turn around and ask them a question: What's it like not to be?

The journey of twins is certainly complex and—dare I say—a single journey. Whether we want to pretend or avoid or dare admit, we are a unit. A unit that is the best of both. We see ourselves in each other's eyes and know we are each other's best version of ourselves. Together we are complete.

My twin journey with Kathy was one filled with so many experiences of laughter, teenage angst, and, the best of all, comic relief. The one story that always comes to mind is during our high school cheering days. We were at a game in a school. Let's just say the girls were far more advanced than any of us were (and certainly let us know that by marking their territory). I, being holier than thou, made a defamatory comment in their direction. In a bathroom environment. Upon making my statement, I threw Kathy in front of me and ran out of the bathroom, leaving her to be fed to the wolves. (Which, by the way, these girls looked like.) I ran to our other teammates and informed them of my sister's predicament, thinking she was going to be taken out by an ambulance with missing body parts.

To everyone's surprise, Kathy walked out of the bathroom looking like a hot mess. I think her cheer skirt was now her top, but no one let her in on that. Her hair: Let's just say it took two days to get a brush through it. But you should have seen the other girl. Wait, I mean girls; I did say plural. They came out of the bathroom crying with ripped clothes and shoes off. I turned around and looked at my sister. Is she a freak of nature? How did she come out alive?

We all ran up to her and asked, "What the heck happened in there?"

Kathy answered calmly, looking at me, "I just pretended they were her."

Crap.

MATERNALLY CHALLENGED

WHAT WAS I THINKING?
MISERY LOVES COMPANY

We left the hospital five days later with Casey strapped into the car seat. That job alone took quite a while, and he looked like ET sitting there. Robbie and I were so out of our element, and it became comical. It took us, like, 10 minutes to get Casey out of the car seat. Let's just say the both of us combined did not make us the sharpest tool in the shed.

The first hour of being at home started this rollercoaster ride of a lifetime. I began to feed Casey a bottle, and all of a sudden he projectile vomited across the room and hit the wall. A little indigestion? Hell no! I had not seen this in the hospital and got really worried. Robbie came up as soon as he heard the words "WTF!" yelled. We both just sat there with glazed and scared faces.

We decided to wait a little while to feed him again. Casey had fallen asleep in my arms, and we just chalked it up to him maybe not liking the house. LOL. Well, that was only the beginning!

As the days progressed, it got worse and worse. Casey could only eat about half an ounce of formula at a time, and it would take about 40 minutes for him to do this. And the sleeping was horrendous! My husband and I would sleep in shifts. We would stay in the bedroom with Casey, and the other one would sleep on the floor in the dining room with earphones on. The reason for this was that all Casey did from 6 p.m. until 5 a.m. was cry. Yeah, you read that right. Sleep deprivation: What a joy!

I think I spent more time with the pediatrician than I did my own family. I went there once a week until Casey was seven months old. I felt like the biggest failure because I couldn't calm down my own kid. The last time I went to this doctor, he and a nurse sat me down in the office. The doctor proceeded to say, "Kathy, I think you need some medication to calm down. There is nothing wrong with Casey." The nurse said, "You are a first-time mother and need the meds." Say what?

As I was driving in the car with a flood of tears streaming down my face, I thought, "Hell no." I decided to videotape Casey trying to go to sleep and how he was from 6 p.m. until 5 a.m. the next morning. I did it and found another pediatrician.

Thank God for that. I made an appointment with the new pediatrician Dr. Chen. My sister came with me, and we brought the infamous tape. Dr. Chen listened to my story, amidst all the gasps and tears and the fact that I hadn't bathed in three days. Honestly, I looked like a bag lady, and smelled like one. She took the tape to her office and watched it.

A few minutes later, the door opened, and I felt vindicated. I was not losing it and making this crap up. Dr. Chen grabbed my hand and said, "I am so sorry for you and that you weren't heard." She proceeded to explain what she thought might be the problem and had her nurses set up an appointment the next day with a specialist. His name was Dr. Michael Fleisher, and he was a kidney specialist.

My husband and I went the next day to meet with Dr. Fleisher. He listened to us, and then took that same tape to his office. He told us what he thought, but wanted to try out this medicine first, even though he did a sonogram on Casey. We valued his opinion and agreed.

Well, to hell with agreeing! A mother's intuition is always right. That night, Casey was the worst he ever was. He was rolling around in his crib with his legs practically up to his chin, and you could see he was in pain. Needless to say, Casey was scheduled for surgery the next day. The diagnosis was that the tube leading from Casey's kidneys, called the ureter, was knotted and kinked badly. So, the bottom line was Casey only urinated once a day. The middle of the night was when he would be trying to go and couldn't.

I felt like I was at the top of a Ferris wheel with my feet dangling, holding on with one hand, and it wasn't coming down. I was so sleep deprived that I never even really looked at his diaper. I was a zombie and just going through the motions. The biggest regret for me is that I should have known.

Needless to say, I went back to the first pediatrician and told him and the nurses what had gone on. They stood there with dumbfounded faces. I then said that no matter how new a mom is, you should *always* listen to her. Back to a mother's intuition.

A LETTER FROM MY MOTHER

I have twin girls, one of them being the author of this book. I had a seven year old son and never thought I would have another child. Surprise: Kathy and Kelly were born in May 1966—a month early. Back in that day, multiple births were not as common as they are today.

We took them home from the hospital five days later and, to be truthful, my husband and I didn't know what to do or where to begin. No help, except my wonderful husband, but he had to go to work in New York everyday. He was a Godsend when he arrived home from his busy day.

We knew we had to take care of this wonderful gift and so I lit my cigarette, got my cup of coffee, and thankfully got into a routine. I weighed about 110 lbs back then and I could take two stairs at a time.

My 7-year-old son was another Godsend. He knew how to take care of them, except changing a diaper. My neighbors were wonderful. I must tell you here that disposal diapers were not invented yet, so I had to change diapers on the clothesline, since I didn't have a dryer.

The girls are now 50 and my husband is gone, but the great memories are still with me. I could tell so many stories, but it would take too much space. I always looked at all of my children as gifts from God. My husband and I were young, so we handled it all ourselves, laughing all the way. I wouldn't trade one sleepless night or one missed meal for them not being here.

When I look at the girls now all grown up and mothers themselves, I am so proud of them. I always feel blessed that this happened to me and my husband. It brought nothing but adventure, excitement, mystery, and fun into our lives.

How lucky we were to have had the "twinsels."

ANYONE ENJOY PROJECTILE VOMITING?

Casey had the surgery and for a while the eating was a little better. He started to sleep a little more. I still looked like a zombie, and I think a boys' locker room would have smelled better than I did, dirty socks and all. If my husband had gotten a girlfriend during this time, I would have applauded him and said, "Good for you!"

Like most moms know, the introduction of baby food is like doing brain surgery. There are certain foods you introduce first, and then progress from there. I so could not keep it straight. I felt like I was in science class, and let's just say it'd never been my forte in school. At first, Casey seemed to do pretty well, but I saw that texture was going to be an issue. That was the least of the problems. The throw-up rollercoaster ride began with a force!

Every time Casey ate, he would projectile vomit and literally hit the wall. Linda Blair in the movie *The*

Exorcist would've shaked in her boots after seeing Casey. I lived in clothes with vomit on them. After he would get sick, I would sit and rock him and hold him and think, "What did I do wrong in a past life for my child to suffer like this?"

I eventually set up an appointment with an allergist. Naturally, it was some moms at Casey's playgroup who suggested I do that. Someone else had to tell me what to do. You know, the perfect moms who have this down pat. Their kids were eating and growing and sleeping through the night. I would look at them, and they seemed to have these halos around their heads.

Poor Casey! He was the one struggling and never seemed to be hungry. With parents like us, how could he not be hungry? We loved food, and we were not petite people by any means. So, I put on a different mindset and got on with it. I became a warrior mom, and that's when I started to use humor to cope. My philosophy was that I would rather laugh than cry. If I really thought about those seven months, I could cry for hours!

Hallelujah! The allergist appointment was enlightening. It seemed Casey had an assortment of food allergies. I probably should have realized that when his head would spin while eating. He had been on the formula Nutramigen (common for kids with allergies), which should've been a sign. We found out Casey was allergic to the normal: eggs, wheat, soy, and milk.

Moms whose kids have allergies know this one thing: Feeding time is like preparing for a war zone. You cross your fingers and hope the food will not come back up and no more allergies appear. We were good for awhile, but the local allergist suggested we hit The Children's Hospital of Philadelphia (CHOP). In all the years of practice, this doctor had not seen the extent that Casey was allergic to. At this point I wouldn't have been surprised if he was allergic to me.

So the trek began. We met with Dr. Pulaski at CHOP and started the testing all over again. They did the tests on Casey by pricking his skin with the things that make kids have allergic reactions, from food to trees to dogs and cats, and so on. Casey's numbers were so extreme, Dr. Pulaski told me to carry the EpiPen always and to keep a journal of feeding time. After the testing was done and toddler Casey was blown up from the allergies, he said to the doctor, "Thank you." He had been on a table for about an hour, having reactions galore. Dr. Pulaski looked at me and said, "What a great kid. No one has ever thanked me after doing this." You know you're a Chlan when you thank someone after they make you feel like crap.

Allergies: Just one more thing to screw up. I am not that organized of a person, but I realized if my kid was going to be okay, I had to pull up my big girl pants and get on with it. I became the best secretary and note taker. Every detail was written down, and I felt like Lois Lane or Rona Barrett. (They were both writers, for those of you too young to recall.)

Casey was coming up on about 18 months now. Our lives had been so consumed with feeding that I missed out on the fact that he wasn't reaching his milestones. He only crawled a little and was not walking yet. We were at one of his play groups, and I just sat there stunned.

I had a glazed look on my face while watching all the crawling and walking going on. Casey was just sitting, not moving and not interacting at all. A weird feeling came over me. One mother said, "Oh, look. Casey hasn't moved at all." I proceed to say, "Oh, I tied him to the floor," of course using humor to hide the fear that was engulfing my insides. The kids were babbling; silence from Casey.

At that moment in time, I had what I feel like was an enlightenment moment. I knew Casey was different, and I was going to do everything in my power to make it okay. I was going to go to whatever doctors I needed to go to. I have never shied away from a fight. Just ask my sister!

Around this time, Casey finally started walking. The words came soon after, but when he was around other kids his age, you could see the difference. He would just sit and watch and not do anything.

The feeding became a problem again, so I sought out a feeding program. My pediatrician gave me the number of a feeding program at St. Peter's Hospital in New Brunswick, NJ. I called and got us an appointment with the specialists.

I got up the next morning, got Casey dressed, and headed to our appointment. We went into a room filled with toys and chairs and cute pictures on the wall. I thought to myself, "Where is the food?" It seemed children with feeding issues have other issues going on.

The specialist sat down, and Casey sat on a chair at a table filled with toys. She proceeded to ask me a million questions, and then she started interacting with Casey, picking up toys and touching him with them. My first thought was, "Are those clean?" LOL. As soon as anything came near Casey, he pulled away. He couldn't take the touch or feel, and seeing that answered a lot of my questions.

Long story short, they felt Casey was eligible for Early Intervention. This would mean he would go to a school two times a week until he was three years old. Then, at three, Casey would go to a pre-school handicap program from nine a.m. to two p.m. at one of the schools in town. There, he would get occupational and physical therapy, plus have learning time in a class with about nine other kids.

On the ride home from this appointment, I began to sob in the car. I was so overwhelmed with the eating issue, and now they were throwing something else on the plate. I didn't think I could handle it.

I always thought I was a strong girl, but when adversity is thrown at you double time, you kind of rethink things. I realized I was not really sobbing for myself, but for Casey. What would these issues do to him? I knew he was just a baby really, and people always say kids sometimes outgrow certain issues, but it still crushed me. I knew it was not life-threatening, God forbid, but it didn't take away the impact.

I got home and sat my husband Robbie down. At first, he had this glazed look on his face. After what seemed like an eternity, he said, "Okay, Kath, you have five minutes to lose it. Then, we will pick ourselves up and get on with it. We have to be positive and strong, so we can teach Casey to be." I couldn't have loved him more. Laughter and strength became our mantra.

A LETTER FROM MY BROTHER

We all have childhood memories of our siblings. I have identical twin sisters, Kathy and Kelly, who are seven years my junior. They have very different personalities and, as they have aged, no longer look like twins. This particular memory is about Kathy and takes place in the early 1970's when she was maybe in kindergarten or first grade. Getting three kids off to school each morning is always a fast-paced rush and can be stressful for any parent. In our case, it was off the charts stressful due to my sister Kathy's demonic reaction to the clothes she was wearing on any given morning. Things would be going along fine, we all got up for the day, got dressed, ate breakfast all quite normally. But then, as if Kathy was suddenly possessed, she would launch into an angry tirade about the clothes she was wearing. Usually she would fling herself around the floor while tearing off her outfit. This would go on for such a long time that most days my mother barely got my sisters off to school on time. She would change her outfit multiple times all the while screaming, yelling, and flinging herself on the floor time and time again. She would even throw in a few expletives for good measure. Quite surprising for a five or six year old to have such command of adult curse words, while using them with such precision.

I believe Kathy would have to thank me for being there on the raucous mornings, as I can honestly say I saved her life a number of times. My mother, who by the way is not what you would call a morning person, came close to committing bodily harm to a kindergartner on more than one occasion. I would need to position myself between my mother and sister in order to prevent my mother from doing something she would regret, but Kathy would have certainly have deserved. I think I remember my sister Kelly cheering my mother on to give Kathy a healthy dose of whoop ass. The neighbors had to hear this riot every morning as we grew up in a Cape Cod style house that were built very close to the house next door. It's a wonder the police never showed up as Kathy would howl like a wild and wounded animal for what seemed like forever.

It amazed all of us, this strange and weird transformation she would allow herself to become—all over clothing. If I remember it well enough, I think my mother laid out my sister's outfits and that Kathy took issue with it. Maybe because my mother dressed the twins identically. I do think that rubbed Kathy the wrong way. If there was YouTube back in the day and I was able to record the daily tirades, it would have more hits than I could imagine.

After repeated violent changes of clothes Kathy would finally exercise herself back to normality. She must have been exhausted after all of this because I sure do know the rest of us were. She would then merrily go off to school only to repeat the tirade the next day. I don't know how long this lasted or if it still does. Would a 50 year old still act like this over clothing?

LET'S RIDE ON THE LITTLE YELLOW
SCHOOL BUS

I will never forget the first day that infamous school bus pulled down our driveway. Thank God my sister Kelly was there. Our plan was to follow the bus to the school and see Casey get off.

Casey was dressed in a cute little baseball outfit—the Yankees, of course. He had his little backpack on his shoulders. He didn't appear to be afraid, but I could not really fathom that I was putting my child at three years old onto a school bus. I just needed to remember to exhale.

The aide on the bus strapped Casey into the car seat, and the bus pulled out. I quickly ran into the house and grabbed my car keys. My sister and I jumped into the car and followed closely behind. Thank God Casey was the last pickup in the morning, which also meant he was the last to get home. I hadn't really processed that fact yet.

The bus arrived at school, with the teacher, Mrs. Barksdale, waiting on the sidewalk. Off came Casey, smiling and grabbing Mrs. Barksdale's hand. I let out the longest breath of my life. So far, it appeared to be a success.

But as the days went on, when I put Casey on the bus, he would be hysterically crying. It broke my heart, because he was so little sitting in the seat. A little girl named Natalie sat next to him every day. Finally, one day Natalie whispered in my ear, "Don't worry. He stops crying as soon as we get to the top of the street." The little manipulator—God love him! I will be indebted for life to Natalie for letting me eat my donut without any guilt!

After about a month, the calls started from Mrs. Barksdale. She was my rock and my angel, and I will forever be grateful for her. Any teachers that work in self-contained classrooms are gifts from God. This is a calling, and they should make a hell of lot more money than they do. They are helping shape your child.

Casey seemed to be having meltdowns and crying jags that started to last quite a long time. Mrs. Barksdale was intent on breaking this cycle, and I was all for it. This was also going on at home, mostly at mealtimes. The eating issue was still there and appeared to be getting worse. The pediatrician informed me that Casey was not meeting a lot of his milestones and was underweight. Really, did he not think I knew that?

The Rock, as I will call her, informed me that she was also going to potty train Casey. When a child has developmental issues, a lot of skills appear late. They get there, but at their own pace. I was THRILLED! I had someone who was going to extend their hand and help me.

As I told you all previously, I am not an organized person. It was enough for me to keep track of feeding times, but to alleviate some of the pressure of potty training was epic!

The Rock put a strategy into place, and my husband and I followed it at home. We were all for doing what the professional told us. We were so new to this and green as hell.

Dinnertime sometimes felt like a war zone, especially when grandparents witnessed it. While we would all be eating, Casey sometimes would be rolling back and forth from wall to wall. Yes, you heard me right. If he didn't want to eat, he was removed from the high chair. My parents, needless to say, were utterly appalled.

My father especially would go to pick him up, and I would say, "I will cut your heart out." Most of the time, we would laugh after that, because we would all want to cry. My mother would have a comment like, "Kathleen, I have never eaten at a circus before." My response was, "Well, you are definitely the ring leader."

During this time, The Rock thought Casey should have his eyes checked. At three, I thought he was too young, but okay. Sure enough, the poor kid's vision was bad, so Casey got glasses, the biggest pair I have seen on a little kid's head. As we were riding home, with his glasses on, all my husband and I heard was, "Wow." I turned around, and Casey was looking out the window. "OMG," I thought, "the kid probably couldn't see all this time, and that is why he never moved from the spot I put him in!" I have my "Mother of the Year" award on my mantle.

My sister came over, and Casey was staring at her like it was the first time they had met. Kelly asked him, "Casey, do you think Aunt Kelly is pretty?" His response was, "No." I burst out laughing, because we are twins, then I thought, "I guess Casey thinks I'm ugly too." What the hell!

As time went on, Casey flourished at school. Mealtimes started to get a little better, but his allergies became worse. As more food was introduced, it seemed Casey shut down. He would only eat certain foods every day. There was absolutely no variety whatsoever. It became pretty easy for me, but I worried whether he was getting the right nutrients.

The Rock eventually potty trained him, and we had a party. I never thought that would happen. The littlest things made me so happy. He was three-and-a-half years old, and that accomplishment meant the world to me. My friends didn't get it. I think most of their kids were out of diapers at age two. They would yell at me and say that Casey was just lazy. Yeah, right.

People whose kids don't have developmental problems will never get it. You could tell them until you were blue in the face (and my face constantly looked like Violet Beauregarde's in *Willy Wonka and the Chocolate Factory*), but either it just never connected or they couldn't care less.

Casey was beginning to learn colors and numbers, and it was so nice to watch. He was drawing pictures and had physical and occupational therapy to help with his fine and gross motor skills. The day he sat on a little bike and started to pedal was unbelievable!

As Casey made little strides, my husband and I got into a pattern and followed every strategy. Unfortunately, the bottom was going to be pulled out from under us very quickly.

Casey was three, and I put him to bed in his crib. Yes, we still had him sleeping in a crib. It took me ages to get him to sleep through the night, so whatever worked. Morning arrived, and I went in to get him. What I saw almost put me over the edge.

I walked into his room, and Casey was standing up in the crib. All around him was hair from his head that he had lost overnight. There were bald patches on his head. There was hair everywhere. I ran and got the phone and left him in the crib. I called my husband and said, "Get here immediately."

When Robbie arrived, he walked into the bedroom and just stared, dumbfounded. My husband has never been at a loss for words, but this stopped him dead in his tracks. Casey was smiling, and I pinched Robbie to talk to him while I called the doctor.

I contacted the geneticist at CHOP that we had seen the week prior. She told me to gather the hair in a bag and come down to Philadelphia. We did just that. I cried the whole way down, and Robbie just had this blank stare, like he was stoned or something.

The doctor could not believe it either. She admitted Casey and ran all kinds of tests. All these smart and brilliant individuals were at a loss. I would so want my money back from all the prestigious colleges they went to.

Come on; Casey again was an enigma. Really? What did my husband and I spawn?

They told us he had alopecia, which is the loss of hair, but usually something causes it. That is what was baffling them. They felt he had an autoimmune disorder, and I immediately went to the guilt side. I should have breastfed him, but my milk never came in. Maybe I should have hired a wet nurse.

This was only the beginning of a rollercoaster ride I never thought I would be riding. My husband informed me I loved rollercoasters, and I would probably do any extreme sport. I just knew I had to wear a really big helmet! But what about my hair?

ONE MORE LETTER FROM MY MOTHER

I moved to Belmar almost two years ago to live with my daughter and her family. I have two grandsons that live here with us. One goes to college and lives away. My other grandson who lives at home with us is considered a "special education student." I like my friend Ed's term: Just a step behind.

Casey is kind, caring, smart, considerate, and, most of all, has a great sense of humor. He rides his three-wheel bike all over town and at times even rides into Asbury Park. As he goes along he takes pictures of the beach, sunset, etc.

Casey has a dog named Mollie, a wheaten terrier. This is definitely his best friend.

When Casey rides his bike, he always goes to feed the ducks and the swans over at the lake. Sometimes Mollie will run alongside him, but funny as it is, she always returns in the basket because she is tired. It is really a fun sight to see.

I , as his grandmother and friend, wonder how someone who has had so much adversity and disappointment in his life, since he was born, can be so concerned whether the ducks are getting fed. He cares about someone who, or something that, can't help themselves. He has even named some of the ducks and swans. We always make sure we have bread for him to feed them.

If you drive past the lake in Belmar and you are real quiet you may hear the ducks saying,"I wonder where Casey is?"

AND HERE COMES THE FOOD THROWING!

At the hospital, the doctors did all kinds of tests and decided that Casey needed to eat. He was not "thriving," they said. Did they think I was stupid? I just started to laugh out loud, and they looked at me like I was having some sort of fit. I knew he wasn't "thriving." I saw it every day when I was with my girlfriends' kids or when I saw him at school.

They suggested we start coming twice a week for feeding therapy. It was an intense therapy, and the success rate for kids who refused to eat was very high. We were at a Children's Hospital, and I said, "Yes." The school was so supportive, and so was The Rock. It wasn't like we were taking Casey out and cruising the town.

A week later we started the trek to CHOP, which is an hour away from home. By the end, I could do the drive in my sleep. We went into this little room with blank walls, and it felt so depressing to me. I thought, "What the hell?" The therapist explained to me that they don't want any stimuli around to confuse the kids. Okay, but what about the parents? Who is to say we didn't need a little escape? Couldn't you have put a good-looking model on the wall so we could fantasize that we were with him?

They put Casey in a high chair and gave him a few toys. The therapist knew all about the allergies, so the food was approved by the allergist. They started with baby fruit. They put the spoon in Casey's mouth, and all he did was spit it out. So, there went the feeding rollercoaster!

It seemed every time some new food was introduced, Casey shut down. I think the poor kid had projectile vomited so much that he was only going to put the food in his mouth that didn't make him puke. I had to give him kudos for that. Who the hell would want to eat if all you did was puke? We did this for about a month. Like I said, I could do the drive to Philly in my sleep, and the worst part was that every time we went I got pulled over by a state trooper. I am going to confess something that I am so not proud of.

When the trooper would pull us over, I would make Casey take off his hat. I know, it's awful, right? Mind you, Casey had alopecia and was bald. I thought once the cop would see him, he would let us go. It worked like a charm every time. I know, WORST MOM EVER! We didn't have a lot of money at the time due to paying doctor bills, so I didn't need to get a friggin' ticket.

If there is a comical thing about it, it would be that after some time, I didn't even have to say anything. Once Casey saw the lights, he would immediately take the hat off and laugh. God bless him! I was teaching him to scam.

The team of doctors at Philly decided that Casey needed intensive feeding therapy, meaning we would live at the hospital for two to three weeks at a time, and then go home for a few weeks and see how Casey progressed. He would attend pre-school with his IEP intact while we were there. The teacher at Philly would correspond with The Rock and vice versa. Casey would not miss a beat.

To be perfectly honest, it was a very lonely time for my husband and me. We would meet on the NJ Turnpike at a rest stop and catch up. I would stay during the week, and Robbie would go on the weekends. Robbie felt I needed a break or I would go nuts.

During the feeding therapy, it was awful to watch. I would watch from behind a glass and observe the therapist. Casey would be screaming and hitting and throwing things. One day, instead of crying, I burst out laughing hysterically. The poor therapist had a variety of food in her hair. It was a smorgasbord! I decided then that I needed to keep the laughter going or else I would have a nervous breakdown. And believe me: I would need the laughter.

When Casey was little, one of the many doctors we saw was at Johns Hopkins. The geneticist at Philly said we should go back there and get a second opinion. The doctors asked my husband and me all kinds of questions about our families. Prior to the appointment, they had mailed us some of the questions, so we asked our parents to help us with some of the genetic history of our families.

Okay, we got all the info from our families. To say they were not happy was an understatement. My mother's response was, "I am lucky I can remember to put on my underwear in the morning." All right then!

We met with the geneticist; for the life of me, I cannot recall his name. All I know is he was quite handsome. That chiseled jaw was a welcomed distraction to all the worries in my brain. Let's call him Brad Pitt; that is who he looked like. Get on with it, Brad, and tell my husband and me what the hell we spawned.

Brad began asking the questions, and it appeared we were raising our hands for the first few. After some time, I noticed my husband smiling, because Brad was looking at me and saying, "Kathy." I thought he was just enamored with me, but then I realized it was just me raising my hand. Laughter filled the room. Even Brad was laughing. I couldn't stop. I never thought I would be here talking about my family history, and, boy, was it messed up! Then, I told my husband to just lie and say "yes" to some. His response was, "I should have had you checked out before I married you."

They proceeded to take blood from me, then my husband, and finally Casey. They told us to go out for something to eat and come back. We had already been there for about an hour and a half, so we left to go eat.

After some time, we went back to meet with Brad, who proceeded to tell us that at conception one chromosome didn't go to the right place for Casey. He started to talk medical mumbo jumbo, and my husband asked him to make it simple. We both weren't that smart. He said that us together, our genetic makeup, was not a good match. Seriously, now you tell us? Okay, maybe one child would be enough for us. For God's sake, God really laughed that time. Brad told us that one chromosome was, like, dangling and not fully connected. That was pretty much layman terms for us to understand. To this day, I still don't fully get it. I only attended Rutgers University. Maybe I attended too many frat parties and should have paid more attention in class.

When we got home, I told my mother what happened. I informed her that I was raising my hand for most or all of the questions. Silence, and then she says, "Well, that's all your father's family." Maybe she should have checked out Dad before she married him.

LET'S SAY "HI" TO EINSTEIN

I was raised Catholic and went to Catholic school. I learned early on that God has a plan for us. Well, I didn't appreciate His plan whatsoever! After we arrived home from Johns Hopkins, I began to get sick. I would violently get sick, morning and night.

At first, I thought it was karma, how I was using Casey to get out of some speeding tickets! I mean, I was on the pill and had been for almost two-and-a-half years. No way could I be pregnant again. But then dread filled my mind. About two months prior, I had had a sinus infection and had taken antibiotics. Really, could I be in that minority again?

Driving my car to CVS to get a pregnancy test, I begin to hysterically laugh. As you can see, I used laughter so I wouldn't cry. I am not a pretty crier. To those of you out there who also are not, you know what comes out of your mouth and nose. It is not human by any means.

I arrived home and headed to the bathroom. I peed on that lovely little stick and just sat there with a glazed look on my face. After the time allotted for the results, I picked up the stick and gazed at it. I laughed and cried at the same time. Snot and tears mixed: a lovely sight!

I was pregnant. Was God really blessing me with another child? Wasn't he looking down and seeing the "stellar" job I was doing with the first one? If I could have telephoned upstairs, I would have reamed God a new you-know-what.

The funny thing about this was that my husband had had back surgery during all this chaos with Casey, and he was in a back cast. Robbie had this smile on his face when I told him, and he said, "Okay." Okay, really? He said it must have been meant to be. What the hell? Haven't you been sitting in the seat next to me riding the same rollercoaster? How are we going to fit another person next to us? Plus, our gene pool was not good!

We told our families, and my mother got this look on her face. She said to me, "Kathy, you are a dirty girl. Your husband is in a back brace. Couldn't you have left him alone?" OMG! So, in the meantime, Casey was doing the feeding therapy, but he was still not "thriving." His doctor at CHOP, Dr. Maller, suggested another option.

He wanted to insert a feeding tube for Casey. He felt Casey was not getting enough nutrients because of his lack of eating. Casey would be hooked up to this machine for twelve hours a day, but he still had to eat food; this was not in place of eating, but to make sure his body would get what he needed.

It was just another obstacle for Casey. My husband and I talked about it, and our philosophy was to always listen to the professionals. All the doctors we dealt with were always so knowledgeable and kind to Casey. Like my husband said, "I didn't go to med school."

So, as I was heaving out the car window, we headed to CHOP for the feeding tube to be put in. We told Casey that the doctors would put him to sleep, and when he woke up there would be a "button" on his stomach. My kid didn't even bat an eye! Kids are so resilient; it is the adults who freak the hell out.

During the surgery, the doctor's team instructed my husband and me on how to do the feeding. The formula was in a bag on an IV stand, and you just opened the "button" and attached. Easy as pie, right? Well, they told us to make sure it was attached, because if not, the formula could spill out, and they said the smell was not that nice. Okay, when our kids throw up, it is Robbie who cleans it up. I upchuck right next to them. I have a weak gag reflex, and, girls, that is a good thing for me. LOL.

Casey came out of surgery and woke up. He looked down at his belly and said, "Hi, Einstein." My husband and I laughed. He named the "button," and we realized that was how he was going to get through this process. Casey's IQ is 67, but he is the smartest one out of all of us. I think, as time went on, I realized that maybe it was a good thing that he was still little and going through all of this. Casey didn't know any different. Maybe, if he was older, it would have been a nightmare, because he would have known the difference.

So, we headed home from the hospital and prayed that Einstein would help him "thrive." It was tough at first for me. I had to mentally prepare myself that for 12 hours a day that Casey needed to be hooked up to a machine. Of course, he would be hooked up right after dinner and while he slept. But, like during the summer months, he would likely not be able to play after dinner.

It became a routine for us. Dinnertime was still an adventure, but the anxiety was gone for me. I knew he was getting vitamins and nutrients. He seemed happier and calmer, and all we did was laugh! Casey has a great sense of humor, and I am thankful for that. Of course, my mom takes credit for that!

The nausea subsided, and I was starting to feel like myself. The hospital ward in our house was getting calmer. My poor husband! Throw-up and feeding tubes galore would make anyone head for the hills. I still told my husband that if he wanted to get a girlfriend, I was okay with it. "Just check her gene pool," I said.

Casey and I still traveled to CHOP two times a month for feeding therapy. I would sit behind a glass and observe. I felt like Casey made progress and then took two steps back. I felt bad for him and couldn't understand why he didn't want to eat. Was he so scarred from all the throwing up he did? I mean, it was the like *The Exorcist* for him. He would projectile vomit so badly that we would yell, "Duck!"

In the meantime, my husband and I found out we were having another boy. At first, I was a little disappointed, but then I thought about what I had put my parents through with me. I was hell on wheels. In kindergarten, my mother would have to sit on me to put my clothes on. I hated wearing dresses, but my twin sister didn't, so guess who won? I would scream and cry, and my brother would yell to my mom, "Don't kill her!"

When I told my sister that I was having another boy, I said, "What if my daughter-in-laws don't like me?" Her response was, "They probably won't, so just let it go now." Nice, right?

Casey was progressing in school, and The Rock loved him. She was an angel sent from heaven for us. He would smile coming off the bus with his little backpack on his back. He was learning to color and hold a pencil and his ABC's. I felt like maybe the rough waters were subsiding. We still traveled to CHOP for feeding therapy, but Casey still had a hard time with that.

I wondered when this was going to get easier for all of us. It wasn't life-threatening, but I felt like all our energy was focused on food. Now, mind you, I could eat like a man, but I felt that we were missing out on so much of life. Boy, I wish I had kept my thoughts to myself, because again life was throwing us another curveball. And I definitely needed my Depends for this, because I couldn't stop laughing.

A LETTER FROM MY HUSBAND

Casey is my best friend and my hero. I am very fortunate to call this person my son.

Just like Dustin Hoffman played the world's most favorite character in *Rainman*, Casey is my Rainman. When God blesses you with a child, you can't fathom the journey you will be on. The one Casey has brought to us has been a challenge to say the least. It's hard to watch your child be left out, behind or forgotten only to see him grow into a wonderful, caring, loving, and inspiring man. He makes me a better man. I hope when I grow up I'll be just like him.

At the end of the movie *Rainman*, Tom Cruise's character became a better man because of Dustin Hoffman's character. My son Casey has given me an incredible gift: the gift of realizing it is okay not to be perfect!

COULDN'T YOU HAVE STAYED IN THERE UNTIL YOUR DUE DATE?

During my second pregnancy, Casey and I still traveled to CHOP for his feeding therapy. One of the times, the doctor informed me that we needed to do another two- to three-week visit. He felt that Casey wasn't progressing as he should and that a longer visit would do him good. I guess as the kids with feeding issues get older, it is harder to introduce new and textured food. Well, they were in for a ride with my son, a German stubborn streak a mile long. The thing with Casey was that he would smile as he threw food at you. He would have been a great character in the movie *Animal House* during the food fight scene. He only ate the food that never made him sick. Get your ponchos on, people!

Now, mind you, I was coming up to about thirty-one weeks pregnant. I felt huge, but had no worries that I wouldn't go full term. Never did I think I would go early or anything. Robbie and I did what we did best: I would go to CHOP during the week and live there again, and he would come on the weekends. This was about the sixth time we had done this. We were old pros at this and didn't seem to bat an eyelash. The fact that I was pretty big and probably would get no sleep was the least of our problems.

Towards the end of the second week, I started to feel like crap. I knew what contractions felt like, but did not think that was happening. Eight weeks early—no way would God do this to me. Didn't I have enough on my plate? I know I can eat like a man, but come on, my plate was piled all the way to the top. Did I want my family visiting me in a psych ward? Wait, I could look at that like a vacation.

So, I called my husband and told him. He said, "Tell the doctors there, and do not drive." So, I did, and it was Braxton Hicks. I was a little relieved, because the thought of driving in pain was not enticing to me. We luckily finished out the second week, and they let us go home. We made a little leeway with Casey; he ate two different kinds of fruit and vegetables. Holla!

Here came my thirty-third week of pregnancy. I was sleeping, and it was, like, 11p.m. My husband came to bed, and I told him to call my doctor. The pains were excruciating. Robbie did, and my doctor said to bring me to the hospital and he will meet us there. I picked up the phone and called my parents to come and stay with Casey.

Now, mind you, Casey had a monumental moment at school the next day: school pictures. I left a cute outfit out and told my mom. She said she saw the outfit and no worries. They would take care of everything. That's what I was worried about.

We arrived at the hospital, and I was admitted. Sure enough, I was in labor, eight weeks early. Really? My doctor tried to stop the labor with meds, and it seemed to have stopped. Boy, was I wrong! It seems like I am wrong most of the time. As the contractions started up again, I looked over, and there was my husband, sound asleep. I wanted to punch him in the face, and so wished men could give birth one time to see what it feels like.

I had a C-section with Casey, but my doctor wanted to see if I could do a vaginal birth. I was glad, but nervous. This baby would be a preemie, and I prayed that he would be healthy. I was fully dilated and got the "okay" to push. My husband was behind my head, cheering me on. I felt like I was at a football game and needed to throw a pass into the end zone. Well, I did it!

Our son Christian had arrived! He weighed five pounds, five ounces, and my doctor told me if I had gone full term he might have been close to ten pounds. What? As soon as Christian arrived, there were, like, five doctors there checking his vitals and other stuff I couldn't see. They then wheeled him to ICU.

After some time, my doctor came back and told me Christian looked good, but his lungs were not fully developed, and he would have to stay in the hospital. I sat there and bawled my eyes out. I asked God to keep him well. I didn't know if I could handle two children with issues. I felt like I was failing miserably with Casey. Well, at least they would be in therapy together.

I was discharged a few days later. Back then, they kept you for a couple of days, and you weren't kicked to the curb with a response of, "Thanks for coming." My husband and I got into a routine that worked well for us. I would go to the hospital as soon as Casey got on his bus. I would sit by Christian and touch him through the incubator. He was so small, I thought, but there were other preemies there much smaller.

Robbie would then come home, eat dinner with Casey and me, and head to the hospital. We had it down to a science, and Casey liked the routine. Unfortunately, another curveball got thrown at us and that routine was shot to hell!

CHOP wanted Casey to come for in-house feeding therapy again for two weeks. They felt he was getting older with no signs of adapting to new food. The doctors felt that window was going to close and there would be no leeway after that. I thought, "Okay, I have one son in ICU and another trekking to CHOP." I realized I had to pull my big-girl pants up and get on with it. The psych ward vacation would have to wait. Which is a shame because I was so looking forward to that.

So, I left with Casey, crying all the way there. Casey kept taking his hat off, then putting it back on. I think he thought my sobbing was the police sirens. I got him to scam, but he couldn't tolerate certain foods. Really, Casey?

I spent the week there, but fortunately my sister worked in Philadelphia. She would sleep in the hospital with Casey two times a week and go to work from there. This was because I wanted to see Christian also. In my mind, I did not want him to feel abandoned. I also didn't want him to have more ammo against me in the future. As I was driving from one end of the NJ Turnpike to the other, I started laughing hysterically.

This could not be happening! Was our gene pool so messed up or was God just a jokester? Like I said earlier, I am Catholic and was taught God is in the driver's seat. Well, it was time for God to be in the passenger or backseat. One day, telling my mom how overwhelmed I was, she looked at me and said, "Maybe Christian needed to get here earlier. He knows he will have to protect his big brother and God said, 'Okay.'" I was dumbfounded. That's what is great about my parents: they always put a positive spin on things.

Christian was in the hospital for three weeks, but finally came home. The thing was that he came home with a heart monitor. Before he was released, my husband and I had to go to the hospital to get training about the monitor. Oh, goodie, more equipment! I never got to tell you, but during Christian's stay, I would pump at the hospital. I wanted Christian to have breast milk.

Well, that again was funny. The machine would be sucking really hard, and maybe two drops would come out. Christian would have starved. Even with doing it for some time, apparently my milk didn't come in again! WTH? But the nurses told me to let Christian latch on at home and see what happened. I was ready to be successful.

The day we brought Christian home, Casey just sat there on the couch staring at him. His reply was, "Take him back," like he was a toy and we had gotten him at Toys "R" Us. Casey wanted an exchange. If only it was that easy, my boy.

I decided to try breastfeeding. I positioned Christian on a pillow like the nurses advised, and he latched on. The poor kid was working his ass off and getting red in the face. All of a sudden, the door flew open and Casey yelled, "Eahh!" That was the final straw for me. I know all you women reading this who breastfed their children are moaning very loudly, but I did try. I found out from my mother that her milk never came in either. Again, there is that fabulous gene pool showing its face.

One day, Casey came home from school with a big envelope. It was his school pictures - his first one. I was so excited, and so was Casey. He had this big smile on his face, and I could see he was proud. I opened the envelope and just stared at it. What had my mother done? Where was the cute outfit I had put out for him to wear? Casey was wearing an orange shirt and purple shorts. Does that even go together?

I just sat and cried and laughed hysterically! That was so par for the course. We framed that picture and hung it on the wall. I called my mother later on and asked her why she chose that outfit. Her response was, "Casey wanted to wear it, and I thought bright colors would make him stand out." Was she colorblind or senile? Next, she proceeded to say, "Your father was so upset about putting Casey on the bus. He said Casey couldn't even get his little legs up the steps. He wants to know if they can put a lift on the bus so he can get on?" Sure, Mom, I will get right on that!

One day, I ventured out with both boys to go to Target. I strapped Casey in and strapped Christian in with the monitor attached. We proceeded down the street, and apparently I was not doing the speed limit. All of a sudden, Christian's monitor started beeping, and I heard police sirens behind me. Casey knew the drill and threw his hat off. I had just gotten pulled over.

The cop came to the window and looked in. There in the back was a bald-headed kid and a baby attached to a machine. I asked to get out of the car, so I could check on Christian. Of course, Christian was fine. The cop did not issue me a ticket. I told him, "Thank you," and he said, "Looks like you have enough going on." He then stated that he knew from the past that those machines go off sometimes when you are near a cop who is using a speed gun. Great!

I just kept drudging along, and after six weeks, Christian came off the heart monitor. I still slept with the monitor next to my ear for some time. It made me relax a little and wait for the next ball to drop. Bring it on, because I was surviving.

MEET BUBBLES

As they say, time marches on. Casey was still on the feeding tube, but his variety of food did not change. We still traveled to CHOP for feeding therapy, but the window might have been slammed shut. Casey ate what he knew would not make him sick. He ate only two kinds of vegetables, one kind of fruit, some fish, chicken, flank steak, pork chops, and hamburgers. Cream of Wheat cereal for breakfast was a staple, but sometimes an omelet was wanted. He eventually grew out of his food allergies, but would always be allergic to milk and dairy products. His numbers were off the chart for that. So, like they say, pick your battles.

When Christian was three, his pediatrician suggested going to an Ear, Nose and Throat (ENT) doctor. Since Christian had been a preemie, he had a lot of mucus all the time running from his nose. He was congested all the time and carried around tissues. The doctor wanted to do surgery on his adenoids and tonsils; this would alleviate the mucus. I was on board, because I was so sick of snots. Like I said earlier, my gag reflex is really bad. I would be gagging as I would be wiping Christian's nose. He would look at me with this face that said, "Get a grip."

My husband took Christian for the surgery. It was an outpatient procedure, and all of my friends' kids had had it done. I didn't even bat an eyelash, because I knew it was a common procedure. I so loved that my kid was labeled "common."

The procedure was a success, and Robbie brought him home. He looked so cute and little, but he was not; he was a big boy. We put him to bed and proceeded to sit at the kitchen table. My husband began to smile. I said to him, "What?" Robbie laughed and said, "You are not gonna believe what that kid said to the nurse." I thought to myself, "Holy shit." Christian walked at nine months and starting talking early, so by three it felt like he was a big kid already, even though I knew he wasn't. Sometimes I held my breath to see what came out of his little mouth.

Robbie said the nurse brought in a gown and told him to put Christian in it. He got him undressed and put the gown on with the socks they give you. Christian was lying there thinking he was going on a really good ride in his dream. That is how we explained the surgery to him: you will go to sleep and have a really cool dream. The nurse came in and did an IV in Christian's arm. The kid didn't even blink and watched the nurse do it. He thought it was cool. Next, she brought medicine to insert in the IV to make him go to sleep. She did that and said she would be back shortly so the medicine had time to work.

Robbie was sitting there watching Christian. He was smiling and laughing. My husband definitely thought the meds were working. The nurse came in, and Christian pointed to his penis and said to her, "Look. It is growing." The nurse and my husband burst out laughing. He said to her, "I will be going back to the trailer park I came from." I so could believe Christian saying it, but that was not the best or worst line from him. Christian woke up from the anesthesia and looked at his father and said, "That medicine was good, Daddy." Oh, great, what does that say? Listen, Christian, we only have money for therapy. I don't know how much rehab costs.

It became apparent that the surgery did not help Christian's nose. The crap that still came out was foul! Even the ENT doctor was amazed by what came out when he would suck it from a machine. I would sit in the office and gag while he did it. To him, it was baffling. Okay, another oddball born to us.

After some time, the ENT wanted Christian to have sinus surgery. Since he was a preemie, he felt his sinus cavity was not formed right. What the hell did we know? I know we could have gotten rich if we had bought stock in Kleenex tissues. So, another surgery was performed and he came out of it well.

Yet, his nose still ran like crazy. We were sitting at dinner one night, and Casey, who was six then, said to Christian, who was three, "Pass a napkin, Bubbles." Christian did it without batting an eyelash. Robbie and I looked at each other and burst out laughing. Casey was the smartest one in the house and associated Christian's runny nose with bubbles. There was always a bubble of snot coming out. To Casey, it was not a negative thing, because he loved bubbles.

I never wanted my kids to have nicknames, because I had one and hated it! But I could not stop this one. "Bubbles" stuck, and Casey calls Christian that to this day.

Now, the visits to the ENT with Christian became a ritual. One day, the doctor proceeded to tell me he wanted Christian to get tested for cystic fibrosis. He informed me that the amount of mucus Christian's body produced was not in the normal range. "Okay," I said. "Let's get it set up."

We headed to the hospital to do a sweat test. This test is simple and tells you if your child has cystic fibrosis or not. As I was sitting with Christian, waiting to get called, I realized something: I know that there are a hell of a lot of parents worse off than I am, and I know that whatever is thrown our way, we will handle it. I am not going to be in the "woe is me" category. I will not go to that dark side.

We went home and waited for the results. It was awful, because you want to protect your kids and sometimes you can't! It is the draw, and you have to teach them to be strong. Like my dad said, "Play the hand with dignity and grace." But for me, it was more like you felt like you were failing as a parent. I so had to let that notion go. Fortunately, the results were negative! Christian had to take medicine, like steroids, and it was a waiting game to see if he outgrew it.

Christian is 19 now and had sinus surgery again. LOL. It got better, but not great. At least Bubbles can wipe his own nose. Hopefully this one works! Christian is still cute and my baby.

Bubbles had seemed to take on the "older brother" role like it was nothing, always holding Casey's hand and hugging him. Even though he was only three, Christian took on the role of protector. As you know, Casey had alopecia. One day, in the food store, both boys were in the cart. I only had to get a few things and put them both in there. We were walking down one of the aisles, and there was another mother and child there. Both were gawking at Casey, not with compassion, but with a stare I can't explain. Three-year-old Christian said, "Take a picture. It lasts longer." They immediately looked away.

I was like, "WTH? Where did he hear that line?" Christian put his arm around Casey's shoulder and smiled at me. I couldn't have been more proud. What is wrong with adults? I get kids staring and being confused if another child looks or acts differently, but parents should explain it to their kids. I would rather you ask questions than make my kid feel bad about himself.

Another time, we were at the park with my girlfriends and their kids. Mind you, all the kids were between three and six years old. All of us moms sat at the picnic table, with lunch, of course, and watched the kids. It was a perfectly sized park, not too big, and we had our eyes on the kids.

While my friend and I were eating, she pointed to my two. Christian was standing and holding hands with Casey. There were two other kids, about six years old, standing and pointing at Casey. I went to get up, but my girlfriend said, "See how this plays out."

All of a sudden, Christian moved Casey back. The one other kid pushed Christian. Christian raised his fist and punched him in the face. The kid fell down, and Christian grabbed Casey's hand. I proceeded to run over there, and the other mom did too. I asked Christian what happened, and he said, "They were laughing and calling him mean names." Get ready for the response from the other mom. She said, "Well, we don't want our kids touching where your son goes, like the handles to go up on the slide. We should be informed if he has AIDS." WTF!

I looked at her in the face and said out loud, "This is why the world is the way it is, because of ignorant people like you," and I held my head up high and walked away with my two beautiful children. I don't want to seem like I condone being physical, but at that moment I knew Christian would always take care of Casey. If, at three years old, he knew what bullying was, I was in awe of him. My mom said that Christian never seemed to be little; it was like he knew he had a job to do and he did it.

This next incident I am not totally proud of, but I felt at the time it needed to be done. Casey rode to school on a little yellow bus. He got off the bus one day, and my sister was there. I looked at him and wanted to throw up. Someone had drawn eyebrows on him and hair on the top of his head—wait for it—in permanent marker! Casey was smiling and thought it was okay. My sister and I took him into the house and sat him down.

I proceeded to catch my breath and ask him, "Who did this to you?" He said, "Michael." I cringed, because I knew who Michael was. Michael was in the class not because of special needs, but because of his behavior. So I picked up the phone and called the school. I asked the secretary to speak to the principal, her first name being Maureen, and told her what had happened. She set up an appointment for the next day for me and Michael's mother to come in. I was ready with gloves on.

That night, I scrubbed Casey until he was practically raw. It faded, but was going to take a couple of days. I called the pediatrician and informed her, and she said to just do what I was doing. She, herself, was appalled. Dr. Chen actually gave Casey an antibiotic, just to be sure.

The appointment was for 10a.m. the next morning. I arrived and was escorted to the principal's office. I started to get heart palpations, because I had spent many a day in the principal's office in my youth! Maureen and I were just chatting when the door was opened and in came Michael's mother. She was in a fur coat, and her hair was as high as the ceiling: too much Aqua Net hairspray. She gave me a dirty look and sat down. Maureen started explaining what had happened, since she had called the bus company also, and said that Casey was just sitting there quietly. Michael had gotten up out of his seat and started drawing on Casey. Casey had told him to stop, but he didn't.

Michael's mother opened her pie hole and said, "What is the big deal? Just look at him." Maureen couldn't get to me fast enough. I pounced like a lion. I dove on top of her and punched her in the face. Security broke it up. I just wanted to protect my son from the slime of the earth. Of course, no charges were filed against me. I had taken plenty of pictures of Casey and said I would sue for what her kid did to mine. Needless to say, Michael was sent out of the district for behavioral problems.

I am not totally proud of that moment, but ignorant people just need to get their asses kicked sometimes. The apple did not fall far from the tree for Christian. In fifth grade, he won an award for always sticking up for and protecting other kids. Kudos to Bubbles! By the way, wipe your nose.

A LETTER FROM MY YOUNGEST SON

"We ride together, we die together, bad boys for life" is one of my favorite quotes from one of my favorite movies, Bad Boys 2.

But, it also has more of a meaning to me then most could think. That is how I think of my relationship with Casey—he is my ride or die. He knows I have his back no matter what, and I know he has mine. I mean, we are brothers—we do have that bond. But, I have felt a different bond because of him being born a little bit different. He is my older brother and I love him no matter what. To the point where I knew what my first tattoo was going to be when I was about 15 years old. It was going to be a Celtic cross with the words "My Brothers Keeper" inside the cross. I feel this tattoo would speak for me on how I really feel about Casey. It would show that he will always be a part of my life. He will always be involved with my life—when it comes time to have kids of my own, I want them to love their uncle like I do. When people see my tattoo, they understand the message. It shows that life can sometimes be unfair, but that has never stopped Casey from doing what he wanted to do.

Which is why you can say for the most part, he is my motivation for why I wanted to go to college and work hard to secure a future. I wanted to make him proud of me so he can see me being successful. Casey should know I am always here to help him whenever he needs it. I want him to know he has my support in anything he wants to do no matter what it is. We both have always been supportive towards each other, especially when it came to sports. He was at everyone of my football games, basketball games, baseball, it didn't matter what sport. If I had a game, he was there to cheer me on. I was there for him during his baseball career until he decided to retire from the game. My name is Christian Chlan. Casey Robert Chlan is my older brother, one of my best friends and one of the best HORSE players you could ever ask for. I am very proud of him and proud of the man he has grown up to be and can't wait to see what happens in the future for the both of us. More importantly, just wanted to say thanks for being my big brother! I know it ain't easy and I love you buddy.

FEELING HIS OATS

As the years went on, Casey continued to face health obstacles. Another trip to a different doctor informed us that Casey was not growing. They did bone scans and determined he needed growth hormones.

Okay, another battle to fight. He was about thirteen years old, and it had been quiet on the home front for a while. Again, the kid didn't even bat an eyelash. I think, deep down inside, Casey just wanted to be like the other kids and would do anything for that feeling.

My husband says that Casey uses every ounce of his IQ of 67. Being a teenager is rough enough, but for special-needs kids, it can get really ugly. Their emotions are flying normally, but adding in what is going on in their heads is a whole other animal.

So, the hormones were introduced. My husband had to learn how to inject them. I could handle poop, dirt, and blood, but needles just make me woozy as all hell. The funny thing was that after some time Casey did it himself. I know this may sound strange, but at that moment, it gave me a little glimmer of hope that Casey might be able to take care of himself. I think, for moms who have special children, that is the goal.

It is not about going to college, getting a good job, or driving; it is that they can take care of themselves. For God's sake, I have trouble sometimes taking care of myself! Who is with me?

This will hopefully make you laugh. Christian wanted to use a needle to inject himself. He loved needles and wanted to be like his brother! Are you kidding me? My first thought was, "Again with the rehab." Casey, believe it or not, started to grow. I think it gave him a little confidence, and he walked with a little skip in his step. I definitely noticed, because he wasn't wearing Christian's hand-me-downs; I was buying him new clothes. How ironic is it that the younger brother was giving the older brother his clothes? Casey picked out his own clothes with pride. Oh, the little joys in life. Meanwhile, I looked like a hot mess, and you know what I am talking about.

When does it happen? When does it become fact that our children end up looking better than their mom? I mean, I would drive them to school in my pajamas and have the nerve to actually get out of the car! One day, Christian said to me (he was eight at the time), "Mom, please don't open the door. For God's sake, you have Cheerios in your hair!" He opened the door and got out. As I was looking at him, I realized he was wearing the best sneakers and looked really good. I took a peek in the rearview mirror and pulled the Cheerio out of my hair. Yes, ladies, I ate it! The next day, I was dressed and realized sometimes you have to hit rock bottom.

So, Casey entered high school. He was in a self-contained class with a fabulous teacher named Lois Moskowitz. There were about ten kids in the class, and Casey went out to mainstream for classes like art, gym, etc. He seemed to be happy and loved his teacher!

One day, the phone rang in, like, October. It was the school, and Lois was on the phone. She said to me, "Kathy, we had a fire drill, and we can't find Casey." I answered her with, "What?" and began to chuckle. I was not nervous at all, because I knew Lois would never lose a kid. The motto was that no kid was ever left behind.

Lois said she would call back. I am sure they were running around looking for him. I proceeded to call my husband and tell him. Robbie's response was, "Where the hell did he go?" My response was, "You idiot. Everyone will know school is in chaos because of our kid." I've always been conscious of the Chlan reputation.

Lois called an hour later - yes, one hour - and said they had found him. Casey had been hiding in a closet. So, I waited until Casey got home and asked him what had happened.

"Casey, what happened in school today?" His response: "We had a fire drill today. It was raining out. Did you really think I was going to stand outside in the rain? I hid in the closet. Why would they schedule a fire drill in the rain?" Okay, then! It wasn't really raining hard at all. But to Casey, a fire drill at this time was not good. For him to be the smartest one at the school warmed the cockles of my heart. I asked him what he had done for an hour in the closet. Casey said he had closed his eyes and taken a nap. Again, smart.

When your child has special needs, he or she can stay in high school until age 21. Casey said he wanted to graduate at the age of 20, because he didn't want to graduate with Christian. I got that and fully understood. He wanted that monumental day for him to be his own.

You see, when Casey was a senior, Christian was a junior. Their birthdays are both in October: Casey on the 2nd, and Christian on the 5th.

Being in high school, Casey heard a lot of stuff going on, including about the parties and what went on there. We would talk to him about drugs and drinking, and he was hysterical. One day at dinner, my husband asked him if anyone ever offered him weed. His response was classic: "Are you kidding? I can't breathe normally; imagine me having to inhale." God love him.

At the time, Christian was playing baseball, and Robbie and I were at his game. Now, mind you, this was a Saturday afternoon. It was a beautiful, sunny day with no clouds in the sky. We arrived home and headed into the garage, where we had another refrigerator filled with soda and beer. Just to tell you, my husband doesn't drink and hasn't for years. The refrigerator was stocked for when company came over. Robbie opened it and grabbed a soda.

He walked into the family room and asked me if I had drunk a Corona. I said, "No," and then he zoomed to Christian. Christian said, "I was with you, remember?" All of a sudden, Casey walked down the stairs. I zoomed into him, and it was written all over his face. My response was, "Casey, did you drink the beer? And remember, you only have one chance to tell the truth." He said, "Yes."

Casey proceeded to tell us his story. He had heard all the kids in school talking about drinking, and in his words, he "wanted to know what all the fuss was about." As he was walking the dog down a busy street in broad daylight, he was chugging a Corona. Yeah, you read that right: He had the leash in one hand and the beer in the other, and—wait for it—a lime in it.

Robbie proceeded to tell him that he was not legal, that the legal drinking age is 21. Casey just stared at us as I was trying to not bust up. What if a cop had stopped him and asked for ID? Smiling at this time, we asked him what he did with the bottle. Casey said he threw the empty bottle on the grass of the middle school. Not only a drinker, but he litters also. Where did I go wrong?

All of a sudden, the phone rang. I picked up, and it is my neighbor, Marie. I love Marie to death, but she is very serious. Marie told me she saw Casey walking the dog while holding a Corona. She just didn't want him to get caught by the po-po. I told her, "No worries, he told us on his own." Needless to say, it didn't happen again, but I know Casey went into school with a skip in his step.

I didn't know, actually, how I felt about him drinking, but I realized that it was a rite of passage. He had done something that other kids did. The brat never told us, though, whether he even enjoyed it. Casey said it was his secret. Oh, crap. Two rehabs to pay for.

A LETTER FROM CASEY'S TEACHER

Every person wants to have a meaningful and purposeful life. Everyone has hopes and dreams. Everyone needs to learn how to stand up for themselves, understand who they are, make decisions for themselves and be happy. People with disabilities are like everyone else. They have hopes and dreams, frustrations and challenges, want love and friendships and want to be respected. Too often the world sees the disability and not the person. I work to help my students to develop their voice, to understand their strengths and challenges, and to work to give them the skills to move along their own personal path. Casey was one of mine.

In Casey's first year at the high school, he was not put in any classes that I taught, but I knew who he was. He was out there on his own, trying to navigate his school life without the support of a specialized program. He was struggling. I first met him in the lunch room one day because he sat with some of my students. Upon introductions, he moved in for a bear hug and said what good friends we were. I was a bit surprised by his actions because I had never spoken to him before. Anyone looking at us would think that we were long lost friends who hadn't seen each other in years. I moved away and extended my hand for a shake. I told him that since we had never met before, a handshake is how to greet someone new. Casey looked confused. It was clear that Casey wanted me to like him because he was trying really hard to get my approval. His warmth and kind character came out to me even on that first awkward moment and I knew that I wanted him in my classes. I felt that I had something to offer him that would help him not end up in awkward situations like the one we had and not have him stand out. I really hoped that next year, I would have an opportunity to work with him.

As that first year in the high school moved along, Casey's teachers contacted me for advice: How can this young man fit in? He was having meltdowns in classes, he was misunderstanding, the work was too hard, he was running out of class and hiding, he would be clearly upset, cry and refuse to speak. His teachers were becoming frustrated and didn't know how to help him. Casey was clearly overwhelmed and it was getting worse as the year went on. As the academic work got harder, Casey was falling farther behind and he knew it. Coping with this realization became quite difficult for him. It became clear that his current academic program was not helping Casey to learn the necessary skills to make it through his day. It wasn't working and a change needed to be made. The next year, Casey was placed in my class and I was really excited. I felt a change in his program to one that focuses on his strengths would really help him grow and bring back his loving, kind, and warm personality.

My focus for Casey was to help him develop himself. Although Casey had different named classes with me (Careers, Structured Learning Experiences, Life Skills) my objectives for him remained the same: help him learn to understand himself, help him to learn how to cope with life challenges that will come his way, and help him to know that he is a capable person who can succeed. I had lots of fun working with him. He jumped into to activities with both feet. He tried hard to please and to get it right. It took a while for Casey to learn that it was okay if he didn't understand something. This was a hard thing for him to accept. It hit his core. His esteem. He came to me with the misconception that "not getting it" meant he would never get it and it was out of his control. He wanted so much to be like everyone else and thought less of himself because he saw himself as different. I believe that this was the root of many of his meltdowns at the time. I worked hard at helping him learn that it is okay to admit that he didn't understand, and that asking for clarification is a sign of strength, not weakness. Casey excelled in real life opportunities where he could practice his self-advocacy skills. When given practical opportunities to use his skills in meaningful ways, such as helping in the office or working in a kitchen, his confidence rose because his strengthens outweighed his struggles. Rarely did frustrations build to the melting point. He began to be able to identify and talk about his frustrations and be open to suggestions of how to deal with challenging situations. He focused on his strengths. He tried new things. He made new friends and he took more risks. I watched him learn to accept himself and be proud of his accomplishments and of who he was.

Through the years of working with Casey, I saw him grow into a confident young man who could express his wants and needs, understand his disability and how it impacts his learning, and learn to set realistic goals for himself. I believe that Casey learned that his disability would not hold him back from reaching his goals. By the time Casey graduated from high school, he was well on the way to accepting his personal challenges, making decisions that respected himself and most importantly, learning that his voice counts.

THE MAYOR IS ELECTED

As most parents of special-needs kids know, the social aspect of life can be somewhat difficult. I mean, I remember, in the "olden days," how emotional it could be trying to fit in and find a group of friends where you belonged. At times, let's face it, it was hell on wheels!

Robbie and I encouraged Casey to get involved in school. We said, "Be a manager of the football team or basketball," etc. Casey's response was classic: "I'll get right on that," meaning kind of like "f___ you." There would always be a little smirk on his face also, and it wasn't the kind that usually made me laugh. He looked like the Joker from *Batman and Robin*. Not a good look.

One day, Casey came home from school with a packet. At this time, he had been at the high school for 2 years already. My first thought was, "Oh, God, more evaluations." But it wasn't. Holla!

I opened it up, and it was all these forms for us to sign for Casey. He was going to take the plunge and become a manager for the high school basketball team. He informed us that we had to sign the forms for him to return, but we couldn't make a big deal about it. Was he new here? I set off the fireworks!

The journey began. We went to the first game and sat in the stands. It was packed, because the high school team was really good and some of the boys were being looked at by Division I colleges. I looked over at the bench, and Casey was sitting in the middle with the boys around him, holding a clipboard.

I can't explain the feeling that overtook me. My heart was brimming with pride and love; it was a milestone for Casey. He was part of a team. Casey would keep track of all the foul shots for Coach Henning and Coach Motesky. That job was important to the team, and the boys would ask Casey for information at the end of the game.

You know some of those parents who think the Yankees, Giants, etc., are coming for their kids? This experience was so much better for me and my husband than that. Casey was a team member and even wore a varsity jacket!

We would go to every basketball game and could just see that Casey's confidence was growing. I, myself, feel like I don't have a lot of confidence. I'm always trying to please people, basically kissing people's asses to be my friend. I did not want that flaw to be in my children. Casey was standing on his own two feet and loving it.

Casey was the manager for three years. When he was a senior (although he was graduating at 20), they had the basketball banquet. It would be Casey's last banquet, and I felt kind of sad. He said to me, "Time to move on." Good for him, because I was still trying to find myself, and the fact that my son did it before me... Well, enough said.

In the three years he did his job, he was well-known in school, and all the kids were so kind to him. Even though he knew he was different, there were certain individuals who loved him for that. He had a few lasting friendships that were authentic and genuine. I am sure Casey drove them nuts sometimes, since he has no filter, but kudos to the type of girls and boys they were! You know who you are, and I love you for that. If any of you get in trouble, just give me a call. I don't go to jails for visits, though. LOL.

At the last banquet, Coach Henning and the Athletic Director, Mr. Noppenberger, were handing out awards. The first award was a special one. It was for an unsung hero in the name of a boy who had passed away, but had never given up. I had no idea what was going to happen. Coach was talking about someone who came every day and made a big difference on the boys, but mostly on him, making him see the world a little differently. That unsung hero was Casey.

Robbie and I just looked at each other, and the room clapped so hard. I started bawling, and like I said earlier, it's not a good look. I just zoned in on Casey and knew how important this job had been to him. This job shaped who he became, and I am forever grateful for that.

At the end of the dinner, people came up and congratulated us. I said, "Thank you," but knew this was Casey's accomplishment. All the therapy and all the worry had paid off! LOL. Casey had arrived and arrived big.

The next big deal was the prom. I told Casey that I would put on my Spanx, buy a dress, and take him. He was not *not* going to go. He looked at me when I said this, and his response was, "Poke my eyes out and hell no." Out of the mouths of babes. So, I guess he thought I wouldn't look good.

Casey ended up taking his friend's sister, who was a varsity cheerleader. She was a sophomore, and her sister and Casey were friends. So, they all sat at the same table. Casey asked her himself, and they looked great together. My younger son, Christian, was totally impressed, because he didn't have the balls Casey did. I probably would have to take him, and that worked out also. For some reason, I wanted to attend another prom. Glory days.

Before the prom, Casey went to two houses to take pictures. He was around a ton of kids and looked like he belonged there. He was my stud, and every picture taken was with a bunch of girls. I looked at his Facebook account, and it appeared he was a pimp. Christian was jealous. Reach for the stars, boys.

THE MAN HE BECAME

Casey graduated in June, and I couldn't have been more proud. He was sitting in the second row and looked like he had conquered the world. In fact, he had. To think of all the adversity Casey had dealt with and still laughed!

And now the hard work began: what to do after high school, because for most of these kids, this is the only place where they are social. They want to go to the movies, get a girlfriend/boyfriend, and just live. To be frank and no-bullshit, there are limited services available.

Casey would tell my mother and me that he wanted to have a girlfriend and wanted to have sex. As I sat there with a blank look on my face, I realized that he was a typical man. Damn, because I thought he was different and would think with his "other" head. LOL.

For Casey's 21st birthday, he wanted to go to Vegas. He didn't elaborate with me, but informed his father. Was I appalled? No, I thought it was good that he wanted to go to the casinos. Boy, was I wrong!

His father, his godfather, and Casey's best friend (who was a college football player) traveled to Sin City. I knew deep down that this was a monumental moment for Casey. This trip could give him confidence and make him feel "normal." Most of my friends chose to not understand this, because they weren't raising special-needs kids.

I never wanted to actually know what went down, but when Casey got back, he was different. He was a man. I asked him, "So, what did you do?" His candid response was, "What happens in Vegas stays in Vegas." Okay, looks like I am withholding sex from your father unless he tells me. I know one thing they did: took a helicopter ride over the Grand Canyon. No dirty girls there.

Casey attends Brookdale Community College and will be getting a certificate in Culinary Arts. That is a joke to the family because he doesn't eat anything. No strange food ever enters his mouth to this day. A chef usually has to taste test his creations. Casey says he will hire someone to do that for him. My little entrepreneur.

Here is a story about Casey's journey at college. Now, he will not get a "degree" so to speak, but he will get something that will show he completed classes. Last semester, Casey got a letter from the school. I heard him hysterically laughing upstairs in his room.

He came down and handed me the paper. I could not believe it! The kid was on academic probation. We were uncontrollable with laughter. What the hell? Well, Casey had to take the math class three times before he passed it. This was the second time, and things didn't look promising. Casey tore up the letter and tossed it in the can.

He has been at Brookdale for almost three years and is in the math class for the third time. My husband and I really don't care, because he loves to learn and enjoys going to college. I think it makes him feel like the other kids feel. That is his success, and Casey is okay with how long it takes him. I just hope he is not close to 30 before he starts the cooking classes. I need someone to cook in my house. Hurry up, Casey, and get going.

Casey has also stepped out of his comfort zone. He has joined a gym and gotten a trainer. I am a full-fledged gym dropout. I have paid monthly for a gym membership, but I never go. Casey is not going to be me. Thank God for that. He has also been taking piano lessons. To know our family, you would know this is hysterical. Not one of us is musically inclined. I am so tone deaf that my boys banned me from even singing "Happy Birthday." I would lip sync the song.

When he was little, Casey wanted to ride a bike more than anything. He broke his arm twice trying to do it. Casey never got back on a bike until last year. We bought him a three-wheeler, and he absolutely loves it. Casey cruises all over our Jersey Shore town on it. The smile on his face is priceless. It has a large basket in the back, and he puts our dog, Mollie, in it. The scene from *The Wizard of Oz* comes to mind.

Mollie is one of the best things we ever got him. Casey was allergic to dogs, but six years ago we researched and found a hypoallergenic breed that we thought was adorable, a soft-coated wheaten terrier. Casey blossomed with her. He takes care of her, and she loves him to death! When he walks in the door, Casey kneels down. Mollie puts her front paws on his shoulders and licks his bald head. No one loves you more than a dog. A boy and his dog, right?

For those of us raising special-needs kids, our journeys are different, but similar also. There are times of sadness, confusion, desperation, and most of all, exhaustion. I have come to the conclusion that I would rather laugh my ass off than cry.

I have not by any means been the perfect mother. I have my kids' therapy bills I am still paying off, but I hope I made them laugh, and you as well. I wanted to teach Christian and Casey that when hard times happen in their lives (and let's face it, they will), they should seize the day and smile. Life can be a rollercoaster ride, but as long as you hold on, it's worth it.

To my boys, always know that you are my two greatest accomplishments. By being your mom, you have made me the woman I am today. Some will say that I am nuts, but just ignore them. I love you both to the moon and back, and remember: just laugh. It gets you through the day (and a lot of alcohol)!

A LETTER FROM CASEY

Hi. My name is Casey Chlan I am writing to my fans. Here's what this is for: My mom has wrote a book about me and my family and asked that I say a couple things about a topic and how I feel about my family. So here I go. I'll start by defining the Chlan family and use one word and that is Crazy.

We have had our ups and downs. For example, this morning my parents painted the floor of our Florida room and my dad painted himself in a hole. It's been one hell of a ride with me and my family.

As well my family has been through a lot. One way is the point that we moved my parents I thought I was going go crazy. And a family member has joined our house, my grandmother, and she's great.

Okay, so to the fans I hope this will do it.

67820559R00061

Made in the USA
Lexington, KY
22 September 2017